IT'S YOUR BUSINESS

SO WHAT ARE YOU
GOING TO DO ABOUT IT?

Thomas G. Miller

Bonsall, Ca.
tgmgbed@sbcglobal.net

An Innovative Organization for Small Businesses

iUniverse, Inc.
New York   Bloomington

It's Your Business
So What Are You Going to Do About It?

iUniverse books may be ordered through booksellers or by contacting:

iUniverse
1663 Liberty Drive
Bloomington, IN 47403
www.iuniverse.com
1-800-Authors (1-800-288-4677)

ISBN: 978-1-4502-1791-0 (pbk)
ISBN: 978-1-4502-1790-3 (ebook)

Printed in the United States of America

iUniverse rev. date: 7/8/10

TABLE OF CONTENTS

INTRODUCTION

Operating a business is no easy task; 90 percent of all small businesses fail within the first three years. The reason for failure is usually how the business was operated, not that the venture was a bad idea. In difficult times, great management is essential. I learned many lessons the hard way, and these lessons are the basis for this book.

My first job, when I was only ten, was paperboy for the *Oregon Journal*. I was able to develop the route until it was the highest paying route per subscriber in the state. Then came high school in Lake Oswego in the 1950s and that was *American Graffiti* come alive. Next I graduated from Gonzaga University and the University of Oregon Dental School more years ago then I care to remember.

After a hitch in the U.S. Navy, I practiced dentistry in Oceanside, California. During that time, from a germ of an idea I received from an entrepreneur in Minnesota, I created Dental Referral Service with a partner. (I will explain more about this venture later.)

After twenty years in practice, I was ready for a new challenge. I was asked to teach management and finance to small businesses with the Rick Mercer Company in Santa Barbara. I was asked because I had a very successful and profitable practice along with a successful outside business, and Rick wanted me to share this knowledge with others. Over the next five years, I consulted with over 250 small businesses, including dentists, beauty shops, retail shops, laboratories, interior decorators, and a tuxedo rental shop. I even worked with an NBA center— and what an eye-opening experience that was.

During this time I fine-tuned the principles discussed in this book, as I believed they worked in every type of business. I called these principles the SynQuest System. The word SynQuest combines the words synergy and quest and means *a geometrically greater result is obtained by working together*.

All this time, the referral service was being operated by others; and I decided to take an active part in the management of the company. Dental Referral Service's monthly billing doubled four times in next four and a half years. We also acquired the franchise for 1-800-DENTIST in Arizona and Florida. I sold the company twelve years later for about one time gross income.

After I had been retired for about six months, my wife of forty-eight years, Sally, told me, in no uncertain terms, to get out of the house and get a job. That was the impetus for my creating The Kite Depot—The Most Unique Gift Store In The Universe. Three years later, a fire in the shop next door put us out of business, and I retired again.

Over the years, my partner and I created Mail and Office in Portland, Oregon, which we sold. Happily, I can report that it is still in business. We also started Certified Languages, which, as the name implies, is an interpretation and translation business. My partner still operates that business, as of January 2010.

I started another business, licensing the use of the telephone number 1-800-A-P-P-L-I-A-N-C-E to one Appliance Repair Company in each area code across the country. I guess I am not meant to be retired.

Please e-mail me with any comments at tgmgbed@sbcglobal.net. (The gbed in the address stands for my philosophy, *Gettin' Better Every Day.*)

The following are a few quotes for you to keep in mind as you are reading this tome.

The successful business scrupulously follows three basic rules:

Rule I – Expect more than others think is possible.

Rule II— Dream more than others think is practical.

Rule III—Risk more than others think is safe.

—Unknown

The reasonable man adapts to the world;
The unreasonable man persists in trying to adapt the world to himself.
Therefore, all progress depends on the unreasonable man.
—George Bernard Shaw

Listen—learn—lead.
—Unknown

Never confuse activity with achievement.
—John Wooden

"I never give them hell, I just tell the truth, and they think its hell."
—Harry Truman

Superior minds discuss concepts;
Average minds discuss events
Small minds discuss people.
—Unknown

Work hard—laugh often.
—Tim Russert

Chapter 1 - THE BOSS

LEADERSHIP

A friend of mine, who ran what I thought was a successful business, was complaining about rising costs, profit squeeze, poor employees, shabby office, increased competition, and taxes, so I asked him if he was going to close the business. He said, "Of course not! I love what I am doing—I get to be the boss, and nobody can tell me how to do things."

It is true that no one can tell you how to run your business, but properly operating your business will make it a much more pleasant experience along with being profitable. The small businessman, the entrepreneur, is the life blood, the backbone of the United States. Small business hires more employees then all the Fortune 500 companies combined. Small business is the straw that stirs the American economy. So whether you are contemplating starting a business or have been in business for many years, now is a good time to evaluate your business in light of good business practices.

When evaluating your business, it is often best to reconsider the reasons you started it in the first place. Was your primary reason to make a lot of money; to serve people; to give back; to keep busy; you had nothing better to do; or you just like doing this? Whatever the reason, it was your decision to start the business; therefore, it is you who decides what the business is about and how it will be operated.

So, to refresh your memory, right now, on a sheet of paper or on your computer, list the reasons why you want to start or did start the business.

Now that you know why you started the business the next step is to build the foundation for its success.

You are the creator of the business and that makes you the Boss. The boss is the architect, the designer, the generative force; the very heart of the business.

The Boss:
1. Sets high standards—by creating a broad vision.
2. Rips away limits—by challenging the employees to be all that they can be.

3. Gets out of the way— allowing employees to grow through delegation and responsibility.

Ben Gill, an entrepreneur, author, seminar leader, and motivational speaker, says,

> "Of all the tasks implied in the role of business leader, the one that can never be delegated is the role of visionary for the organization. If YOU do not dream dreams, no one will. If YOU are not excited about the future, no one else will be excited. If YOU do not stand at the foot of the mountain and say, 'We will conquer that,' no one will say it."

In his book, *Think and Grow Rich*, Napoleon Hill discusses the characteristics of leadership. He found that all great leaders had a clearly stated vision or set of goals, and they were unconditionally committed to that vision.

To begin building the foundation for the business, four cornerstones need to be laid.

Cornerstone I: Vision and Commitment

<u>VISION</u>

In broad terms, declare how the business will be operated. This is called the *vision* for the business. The word vision is much overused but is a necessary concept. If you do not state what your business is about, your employees and/or your customers will; and their interpretation of what the business is about may not be in your best interests. Only the creator of the business, the boss, the leader creates the personalized vision statement, often called a mission statement, for that business.

For our purposes, vision is defined simply as *a declaration for which there is no proof that it can become a reality.*

We envision it. We declare it. Then we make it happen. We simply declare how the business will operate, and then make the commitment to do whatever it takes to achieve that end.

Tom Peters says that, "without vision there is no result."

YOUR VISION SHOULD NOT BE ACHIEVABLE BY ORDINARY MEANS

On his tape on team-building, Lee Shelton says, "Create goals [vision] by using the S.C.R.A.M. method."

Specific.............Write it down.

Challenging........You need to stretch your limits in order to reach your goals.

Realistic............But not achievable by ordinary means.

Action-oriented....Requires doing.

Measurable.........Must be able to monitor the results.

Once the goal, the end result, is envisioned, develop a game plan to achieve the desired result. Write it down, and as circumstances change, revise the game plan to fit the new facts. By creating goals that are bigger than your expectations, you have plenty of room to grow.

EXCELLENCE IS AN ATTITUDE, NOT A RESULT

"I am committed to excellence and to making a difference in the world through my business."

My wife and I were shopping for some furniture in a very upscale store. The furniture was beautifully arranged, the decorations were impeccable, the help well-dressed and well-spoken. After about half an hour, my wife asked to use the restroom and was graciously shown to it. She was in there for about one minute. When she came out, she said it was time to go, and we left. In the car, I asked her why she had wanted to leave so abruptly. She told me that when she walked into that bathroom after being in the beautiful showroom she saw paint pealing off the wall, liquid on the floor, drops on the toilet seat, a dirty sink, a plunger alongside the toilet, and, all of a sudden, she didn't have to go, but she had to leave. "If they allow their bathroom to look that bad, what else is there that I cannot see? I question their commitment to excellence."

One of the great all-time TV ads a few years ago was one by Standard Oil. Each time a question was asked, the answer was always, "Yes, you can!"

"May I use a credit card?" "Yes, you can!"

"May I use cash?" "Yes, you can!"

"May I use the restroom?" "Yes, you can!"

Anything the customer could ask for, the answer was always, "Yes, you can!"

That sounds like a commitment to excellence to me.

Does your business demonstrate excellence like the first story or like the last story? Are you sure?

Part of any vision must be a commitment to excellence. This commitment begins with being aware of your own excellence and the excellence of your employees. We envision it. We declare it. Then we make it happen. We don't let reasonableness, excuses, or circumstances stand in the way of results. We simply declare how the business will operate and then make the commitment to do whatever it takes to make it happen.

Continually acknowledge excellence in those around you, and, as you might imagine, excellence will happen. Most of us do hundreds of little jobs each day that demonstrate our excellence but largely go unnoticed. When you talk about excellence, others become aware of it.

See yourself and your employees as 10s. Then, experience it. Part of experiencing yourself and your employees as 10s is to talk about excellence.

> "Isn't she great?"
>
> "You are sure a nice person!"
>
> "Didn't he do a super job?"

TREATING PEOPLE WELL IS AN ATTITUDE, NOT A RESULT

"I am committed to treating people in such a manner that they hate to leave the business, because they face a harsher world outside. While customers are in our business they are the center of our universe"

Did you see the movie *Pretty Woman*? Remember when Julia Roberts went shopping and the clerks treated her like a second-class citizen? And what Richard Gere told the manager of the second store? "We need some major sucking up here."

How you feel when you are flying and the stewardesses are talking among themselves while serving drinks? Or what do you think when the checker at the grocery store is talking to the bagger about last night's date while computing your bill? Or when the chef in a restaurant puts out your plate of food and your waitress is talking to the busboy, and your meal sits and sits and sits? Or when you ask a question at the hardware store and the clerk sighs or snickers, letting you know he thinks you asked a stupid question?

How well are you being treated? Are you the center of their universe? If you have a choice, will you return to these businesses?

Now, contrast those examples with this sign that hangs in my dentist's office.

1. We are an on-time office.
2. All possible measures will be taken to see that you are comfortable during your appointments.
3. All procedures and fees will be discussed and agreed to before any treatment is started.

These three statements tell the patient that:

- the doctor (boss) feels the patient's (customer's) time is as valuable as hers
- she cares about the patient's (customer's) comfort (both physical and mental)
- the patient's (customer's) financial considerations will be addressed up-front
- the patient (customer) is vitally important to her.

I told the dentist that these are nice, pretty words, but they mean nothing if they are not the truth. She replied, 'we are occasionally late (the reasons are not important), but as soon as we realize we will be late, all patients involved are told and given the choice to reappoint or be seen as time allows. All patients thank us for keeping them informed, and most stay to be seen.

"Dentistry is occasionally uncomfortable. We go to great lengths to let patients know what to expect from treatment so they have few surprises.

"We always have an agreement from the patient as to the fee charged, and how that fee will be paid.

"When I declare, in no uncertain terms, what the patients may expect, this declaration then becomes the patients' expectations; and the patients' expectations are always met or exceeded.

"The result is that patients never leave the practice except by death or moving too far to commute, and patients refer friends to us because they know exactly how their friends will be treated."

Patients are putting their names on this dentist's mailbox. (See the chapter on Employees—the Bob Gaylor story.) Are your customers putting their names on your mailbox?

PROFITABILITY IS AN ATTITUDE, NOT A RESULT

"I am committed to profitability for myself and all those working for me."

Being profitable is not a bad thing; it is a good thing. You cannot be in business for long if your business shows a loss each month. Likewise, if your employees are poorly paid, you will continually be training new employees and will not be able to give the kind of service that will make your business profitable.

These are big statements. They tell the world what to expect from your business. Once the vision statement is created, the character of the business will begin to develop.

The following are vision statements from
three types of businesses.
THE VISION (our responsibility)
███████████ is a results-oriented, problem-solving
company,
With a staff that provides unreasonable service.

The VISION

███████████ provides a great experience for every person who enters our store.

We treat people like they want to be treated.

Our customer is the most important person in the world while she/he is in ███████████.

Our looks, demeanor and actions demonstrate our respect for our customers.

███████████ is a highly profitable business.

███████████ vision for his dental practice:

We are a source of referral for all quality health services.
We deliver excellence in all that we do.
We are massively profitable.
We share the profit with each other.
We have a staff of people who are all 10s.
We have a happy warm service environment.
We are all involved in winning—patient, staff and doctor.

"I am committed to profitability for myself and all those working for me."

COMMITMENT

Once the vision is declared, each member of the team must unconditionally commit to it. Commitment is what transforms a promise into a reality. It is the words that speak boldly of your intention. It is making the time when there is none. It is coming through time after time year after year.

Commitment is the stuff character is made of. It is the power to change things. It is the daily triumph of integrity over skepticism. Without commitment, a vision is just words.

On a separate sheet or on your computer or on the opposite page, begin the creation of your vision. This will be a work in progress as you work your way through this book; but it is important that you begin putting your thoughts down on paper.

Corner Stone II: CORE VALUES

The second cornerstone is to declare the core values for the business. Declare who you are and what you believe. This step is critically important, because if employees do not know what you stand for, they will not be able to conduct your business as you want it to be conducted. If you do not declare your core values, then employees will insert their values, and their values may not be ones you want associated with your business. You can easily lose customers, because what the business is really about is not evident to the customer. All employees must commit to espouse these values or they are not qualified to work in your business.

Here are some examples of declarations from businesses around the country.

- I commit to excellence in everything I do.
- I commit to treat everyone in such a manner that they will hate to hang up the phone or walk out of our office because they will face a harsher world outside.
- I commit to the profitability of all of our clients, my company, and myself.
- My job description: If something negatively impacts our customers, I am responsible.
- Today is the only day that counts, and no matter what happens, I will have a great day.

Next on a separate sheet or on your computer or on the opposite page begin creating your own core values.

Cornerstone III: <u>AGREEMENTS</u>

The agreements are declarations of how you live in the business. These are the commitments that each person in the business, from the boss to the last hired employee, agrees to live by.

Here are some samples of agreements businesses have adopted.

The Communication Agreement

I agree that, as the speaker, I am absolutely 100 percent responsible for what the listener hears.

Making yourself understood by another human being is a very complicated process. It takes practice, time, and patience to get your ideas across to another; therefore, you must take responsibility for what is heard and not stop communicating until you are sure you have been heard. (See the section on delegation.)

The Sub-Grouping Agreement:

I agree that I will not complain about anyone else in the company except to someone who can do something about it. I also agree that I will not say anything about someone else that I have not already said to him or her.

This is the *no gossiping* or *keep the workplace safe* agreement. I know that, if I see two coworkers whispering, and when I walk up they stop whispering and look guilty, I know that they were talking about me and that they were planning a party for my birthday. A safe place. Gossip is the number one reason good employees are lost.

The No Grumping Agreement:

If I see a problem in my workplace, I agree to find a solution and then communicate only that solution to my team members.

It is easy to bitch and moan about a problem but very rewarding for everyone when solutions are proposed. Either I am part of the problem or part of the solution.

The Responsibility Agreement:

I agree that I am absolutely, 100 percent responsible for the success or failure of this company.

Please see the first section of Chapter 2, under the heading "Is Your Name on the Mailbox?" We are all responsible for everything that happens in our life. We may not be able to explain why something happens, but we are still responsible for its happening.

The Support Agreement:

I will support all other members of the company in keeping their agreements.

Everyone is human, and a person will from time to time break an agreement. That is when the other members of the team must step up and nicely remind the person of the agreement he or she made. Agreements are not just window dressing. They are meant to be our guides to happy living in the business. This is the most difficult agreement to keep because it means that you must let a co-worker know when they are breaking an agreement.

The Let's Get On With It Agreement:

I agree that, if at any time, for any reason, I feel this company is not right for me, I will absent myself from this company. I also agree that, if at any time, the company feels I am not right for it, I may be released with no reasons given.

This should be self-explanatory since all employees should be "at will" employees. Giving a lot of reasons for letting someone go only starts arguments and makes for hard feelings. If an employee quits, the boss knows why; likewise, if an employee is let go, she knows why.

The Golden Rule Agreement:

I commit to treat others as I would like to be treated, even if I am not being treated that way.

This is being willing to turn the other cheek—to go the extra mile.

Now on a separate sheet or on your computer or on the opposite page, begin to formulate your agreements, your statements as to how all employees, including the boss, will live in your business.

Cornerstone IV: <u>MANAGEMENT STYLE</u>

Often, people will not set high enough standards or make lofty declarations because of the perceived difficulty in reaching completion. When you have a problem to solve or a goal to set, what is your process for solving the problem or achieving the goal?

One method for achieving goals and solving problems is to generate a plan for success by working backwards from the envisioned successful completion date to the present. Break down the big job into many "bite-sized" tasks, and set definite dates for completion of each step. Have an employee responsible for each step and set up a reporting system. This procedure of outlining the necessary bite-sized tasks, while time-consuming, will make achieving goals much easier.

The steps for reaching your goals are:

1. Determine the objective.
2. Obtain alignment of the employees.
3. Determine the tasks that need to be completed.
4. Set completion dates.
5. Develop a reporting system.

Are you to be a *manager* or a *leader* or both?

<u>THE MANAGER</u>

- Finds the most efficient way possible to accomplish a specific task
- Is action-oriented
- Keeps "ownership" of the task
- Is oriented toward efficiency
- Enjoys pulling together the details to maximize project success
- Uses influence to get the job done now.
- Relates well to short-term planning process
- Concentrates on output
- Is control-oriented and motivates toward specifics
- Manages things

THE LEADER

- Is sensitive to changing dynamics, maintaining a clear vision
- Has a mission orientation
- Concentrates on empowering others for the task
- Usually keys on effectiveness
- Concentrates on "what" needs to be done rather than "how"
- Uses influence to gain acceptance of the potential for the future
- Is oriented more to having team goals
- Emphasizes "input"
- Is inspirational and charismatic with motivation toward the vision
- Leads people

FOOD FOR THOUGHT

THE GOLDEN POINTS OF LEADERSHIP

Your leadership ability increases when you understand that:

* Your work is done through others

* You need the team more than it needs you

* Your income depends on how well your team members do their jobs!

STAYING FOCUSED AND GETTING THINGS DONE WITH SINGLE-HANDED MANAGEMENT

1. List all the things you need to do today.
2. List them in order of importance, with the most important at the top.
3. Work on the #1 priority item until it is completed, then to #2, etc.
4. Check off each item when completed.

Note: You may not complete your list, but your satisfaction will be great because what you do complete will be high-priority items. If you complete the first five items, you will find that you will have completed most of what was important.

When you see this works for you, have your employees do it.

Save these lists. They exhibit your accomplishments, not your failures.

THE FINE ART OF DELEGATION

Delegation is the act of a leader giving a subordinate the freedom and the dignity to practice becoming better, by assigning responsibility and authority and empowering that person to act for the leader.

When do you delegate?

1. When someone can do the job better than you—let him do it!
2. When someone likes doing a job better than you do—let her do it!
3. When someone can do the job faster than you—let him do it!
4. When someone can do the job more cheaply than you—let her do it!

Therefore, if someone can do it better, faster, or cheaper, let him or her do it!

What do you delegate?

1. List all the things you do.
2. Then, make two lists:
    a. Everything that only you can do.
    b. Everything else.
3. From the everything else list, pick a handful (four or five) that you most want to do.
4. Delegate the responsibility and authority for everything that's left.

How do you delegate?

1. When you delegate a task, give away both the authority to do it and the glory that goes along with its accomplishment.
2. Use language to be sure an employee understands what is expected, without talking down to her. For example:

    "I'm not sure I made that clear. Would you repeat, in your own words, what I said?"

    If she repeats the instructions incorrectly, say:

"What I meant to say was ..." and repeat the process until you are understood.

If a boss can be satisfied only when tasks are done her way, even though an employee's method would produce the same results, you have the makings of trouble. No one likes someone looking over his shoulder making suggestions and demands.

Instead:

- State the vision.
- State the desired results.
- Give a completion time.
- Then, stand back and let the employee produce.

Great leaders all create support groups (a board of advisors) to assist in implementing the vision. Support groups are like coaches, encouraging people to heights they could not reach alone. Many times, a spouse can be a good coach, provided that the coaching is done in a non-judgmental manner.

Cultivate role models, mentors who are successful in business, and ask for their advice. Professional coaching can be helpful, too, but be sure these paid coaches have nothing to gain from the advice they give. Insurance, equipment, and systems sales people all want to be coaches, but all have something to sell, and their advice may be colored by the product or service they are selling.

Your vision, core values, and agreements have now been created. You have determined your objectives. These now need to be carefully explained to your employees. While discussing your philosophy, encourage feedback, answer questions, and have your employees align with you.

Talk is cheap.

Now it's time for action!

Chapter 2 - THE EMPLOYEE

IS YOUR NAME ON THE MAILBOX?

I met Bob Gaylor at a TEC meeting I attended. Bob had achieved the rank of chief master sergeant of the Air Force in 1977, the highest enlisted rank in the Air Force. He was one of only twelve to achieve that distinction. After retiring from the Air Force, Bob began working with USAA Insurance Company as a management development specialist. Bob told this story.

Bob lived in a nice neighborhood, with each house on a large lot. Every Saturday, he and some neighbors would each spend several hours laboring in their separate yards. It was dirty, sweaty, hard work, but they all enjoyed it. One Saturday, on an especially hot day, his wife brought out an ice bucket with a few beers in it. Seeing his next-door neighbor drenched in sweat, Bob walked over to the fence and offered him a beer. It was accepted, and Bob said, "Jim, why do we do this?" And the neighbor replied, "Because our name is on the mailbox."

Have you ever asked an employee at a store if that store carried a certain item and had him reply, "No, *they* don't carry that"; instead of, "No, *we* don't carry that"? This employee, for whatever reason, does not feel he is part of the business; his name is not on the mailbox.

Can you have employees, from top to the bottom, who feel so good about your business that they are willing to put their names on the mailbox? I'm talking about employees who make statements like the following:

"Yes we do _____"

"My company will _____"

"Our business does_____"

Statements that show they have a sense ownership and that their names are on the business mailbox?

The answer is a resounding yes.

How?

The boss takes charge and declares how his business will operate, and it then becomes apparent that the basic job description for all employees is:

* To commit to the boss's vision and goals for the business; and
* To remove obstacles so the boss can:

- set high standards for himself, the employees, and the business.
- dismantle all limits to success.
- get out of the way of employees doing their job.

IT IS THE *EMPLOYEE*	who assists in clarifying our customers' needs.
IT IS THE *EMPLOYEE*	who stimulates a desire in our customers for the finest services and products.
IT IS THE *EMPLOYEE*	who promotes confidence in the skills and integrity of the business.
IT IS THE *EMPLOYEE*	who permits a business to economically thrive rather than merely survive.
IT IS THE *EMPLOYEE*	more than the accountant, banker, or lawyer, who can positively influence the gross and net of the business.
IN SUMMARY -	No single factor in business is a more telling determinant of success in business than the quality of the *EMPLOYEES*. Period.

The boss has the vision for the business, and the employee carries it out. Part of the boss's vision is to have a staff of only unconditionally committed 10's who are givers, accepting of change, and who bring answers, not questions, to the whole process of accomplishing the vision for the business.

THE HIRING PROCESS

Hiring begins with defining what you are looking for. Bob Spence, of Creative Leadership Consultants, calls it the "who, what, ticket, and compensation."

The "who" are the qualities you are looking for in the person you hire.

The "what" are the basic responsibilities for the job.

The "ticket" is what is required in the way of experience and education.

The "compensation" is whatever combination of salary, bonus, and benefits you are offering.

These four points are then incorporated into whatever method you are using to find employees.

If you place a Help Wanted ad, remember that your ad directly reflects you and your business. Give job-seekers a chance to learn something about your business before they apply. Draw attention to the ad, create interest and desire, and ask for action.

The following are two sample ads:

- SEEKING a very special person to staff our business reception office. We value good communication skills, ambition, involvement, energy, and organizational skills. We stress personal development through continuing education, full participation with our team, and strong involvement with our customers. Previous experience not essential, however, we believe you should be personally stable and self-motivated. If you are seeking a real opportunity to grow and fulfill your potential, we think you will find our quality-oriented office an exciting and rewarding experience. Our pay is well above the usual, with liberal health and vacation benefits. Please call 555-555-5555.

- WANTED: SUPERB TEAM MEMBER

  We are seeking a receptionist who can help our team attain a new level of customer-centered effectiveness.

  WHAT WE HOPE TO RECEIVE: A colleague who will bring to our team a quick, eager mind, great interpersonal skills, and personal stability.

  WHAT WE ARE ABLE TO GIVE: A promise that you will work with high-achievers; an opportunity to contribute to the lives of others; a team that is committed to your success and personal/professional growth; active participation in business decision making; above-average financial reward; great health and vacation benefits; and a pleasant business environment.

WHAT NEXT: If you suspect that we could make a real difference in your life and that you could be a real addition to our business; if you feel this may not be just another job, please phone for an interview. 555-555-5555

Another way to find employees is through existing employees who might be given a bonus for finding a replacement employee. Look at employees of other businesses and you might find intelligent, capable, caring, individuals just looking for an opportunity to join a business like yours. You might also ask existing customers who know your business and philosophy. A mailing to your customer base is a good method of announcing job openings and asking for assistance in filling them.

Remember, if you are not getting many good applicants, it may be because all the 10s are already working. Make working in your business so desirable that as soon as word is out that you need a new employee, the 10s respond.

THE APPLICATION (See sample at the end of this chapter)

Note: Even if you are not looking for an employee, always take applications and file them away for future reference. You never know when you will need them.

When applicants call, after getting their name and phone number, ask some specific questions that look for specific answers, such as:
- *Are you currently employed? Yes/No*

- *Doing what?* _____ *(If the applicant is doing, or has done, the kind of work that you will need him/her to do, then give the applicant 10 points; otherwise, 0 points.)*
- *How much experience have you had as (what you are advertising for)?*____ *yrs*

  (Over 5 years: 10 pts; 2–5 years: 7 points; less than 2 years: 3 points; 0 years: 0 points)

Make careful note of the caller's diction and speaking voice.

Voice	10	5	0	*(We are looking for applicants who are clear, easy to understand, using good grammar, are professional sounding, have an easygoing phone manner, and are cheerful.)*
Personality	10	5	0	*(your impression)*

TOTAL SCORE _____

A score of 20 or more: "We'd like you to come by and fill out an application. May I give you directions?" _____ *If yes: "When might we expect you?"*

A score of below 20: "Thanks for calling. If we need to talk to you, we will call."

When the applicant arrives, if possible, have an employee act as a screener using the following criteria:

- Is the applicant's overall appearance pleasing to the eye? Y___N___

- Is he/she neat and clean? (Make careful note of hair and fingernails.) Y___N___

- Will the applicant represent the business in a positive manner? Y___N___

If the answers are yes, give the applicant your application form. (See the sample application at the end of this chapter.) When the form is returned:

- *Did he complete the application 100 percent?*
  - *Yes: 10 points; No: 0 points*
- *Is the application neat?*
  - *Yes: 10 points; No: 0 points*
- *Former employer's section: Did she give month and years of employment?*
  - *Yes: 10 pts; No: 0 points*
- *Average time on the job in the last ten working years?*
  - *Over 60 months: 10 points*
  - *Over 36 months: 7 points*
  - *Over 24 months: 5 points*
  - *Less than 24 months: 0 points*
- *Will applicant be an asset to the office?*
  - *10 — 5 — 0 points*

TOTAL SCORE _____

If the applicant receives 30 points, continue with the interview. Don't spend too much interview time on the applicant's experience. A 10 will learn things very quickly. If an experienced employee is desired, spend about three minutes learning the applicant's level of expertise in the specific job to be filled.

Then spend the most time getting to know the applicant. Ask for appropriate information, and be sure you get appropriate answers. Following are some questions; in parentheses are the answers you are looking for.

- "Tell me your background and education." *(What education or experience has she had to be able to do the job?)*

- "Tell me your greatest attributes." *(People-person; has integrity; is friendly.)*

- "Tell me what you liked about your last job." *(Being included, listened to, and treated with respect.)*

- "Tell me what you didn't like about your last job." *(The opposite of what she liked.)*

- "Tell me what you feel you could bring to us." *(Team player, friendly person, quick learner.)*

- "Tell me the funniest thing that ever happened to you." *(Can she laugh at herself?)*

- "How soon would you be available?" *(Does she feel she needs to give notice to present employer?)*

Have her read something out loud. *(Can she read? How confident is she?)*

If you like the answers, it's time to state your vision, describe your business, describe a 10, Giver, and Offensive Player. Describe Unconditional Commitment and explain your entire vision. Talk about sick leave, vacation, medical insurance, full- versus part-time, dental care. By doing this, you are giving the potential employee a chance to choose to be in your business.

Now, ask her, "What kind of a pay would it take to buy your service?" Then, outline the forms of compensation. The conversation might be something like this: "Judy, if you'd like the job, your starting pay will be $X,XXX. At the end of ninety days, if you really are a 10, as it appears you are, I'm going to raise your pay to $X,XXX. How do you feel about that, Judy?"

If Judy accepts the job, then look her right in the eye, and ask, "Judy, are you committed to my vision?"

There are only three possible answers to that question: "Yes," "No," or "I'm not sure."

1) If the answer is "Yes," say thanks and tell her she's hired.

2) If it's "No," thank her for coming in.

3) If it's "I'm not sure," and you like her, say, "Fine, I'm going to hire you, but only for fifteen days. Then I'm going to ask you again, because as you know, I'm only going to work with employees who are committed to my vision."

Most employee / boss relations

Are poor because the employee

Does not know what is expected.

If you hire from your vision, you are

Going to have an all-10 staff.

EMPLOYEE EVALUATION

Periodically, at least once each quarter, but more often if needed, get together with each employee, individually and privately, to let him know how he is doing.

To determine the quality of your employees, review and evaluate their performance and ability in the following five areas:

OVERALL EFFECTIVENESS

The Overall Effectiveness Review involves an employee's basic job skills and personal appearance. How does the employee perform his job? Does he do the job properly? Does he give 100 percent? Does he present a pleasant appearance?

You are not looking for Jennifer Lopez or George Clooney. Rather, you are asking if your employees are pleasing to be around. Does he make the best impression he can with what he has to work with?

On this overall review, rate employees on a scale from 1 to 10, with 10 being best.

*A **10** is unconditionally committed to do whatever it takes to achieve the company vision, purpose, and goals.*

*A **9** is a 10 waiting to happen and will become a 10 with the proper leadership and guidance.*

*An **8** has the potential to become a 10 but does not yet understand the commitment it takes to become a 10.*

*A **7** is not on the bus. Is more of a drag on others rather than a team player; part of the problem rather than part of the solution; always has to be told what to do; has no apparent interest in bettering himself or the company through his work. He's just there.*

UNCONDITIONAL COMMITMENT

Unconditional commitment is defined as the willingness and determination to do whatever it takes to get the job done. This should not scare anyone. An unconditional commitment to work is as natural and normal as an unconditional commitment to family or church.

When evaluating, consider to what degree this employee is unconditionally committed to your vision? Will he do whatever it takes to get the job done? Remember, employees cannot automatically know your vision. You have to tell them. Unconditional commitment is also rated on a scale of 1 to 10.

THE GIVER VERSUS THE TAKER

This is perhaps the most critical area of all, because a taker can ruin business. By definition, a giver knows that the more he gives, the more he gets. A taker, by definition, feels that in order for him to win, someone else has to lose. Givers give energy. Takers drain energy. Have only givers in your business.

In your review, assign a *G* or a *T* (giver or taker) for each person under consideration.

OFFENSIVE VERSUS DEFENSIVE

This category deals with resistance to change. Everyone resists change to some degree, but the offensive player, when a change is made, takes the ball and runs with it. A defensive player generally digs in his heels and resists the change. In a thriving business, change is continuous, and if an employee is not willing to accept that change, the business cannot move forward.

Sometimes a Defensive player will attempt to wear you down with endless questions. Asking questions is fine; you want everyone to understand. But a Defensive player often uses questions as a tactic to get you to modify a change or procedure to his liking. Eliminate defensive players.

Grade this review with an *O* or *D* for offensive or defensive.

THE SUPERSTAR

The Superstar is the person with the vision, therefore the boss. If an employee is a superstar, it is not a term of endearment. That's because superstars are following their own vision, not the boss's. Almost always, superstars have the business revolving around them rather than around the boss's vision. They also tend to "develop" their jobs in a way so that no one else can do them. Never tolerate a superstar in your business.

The grading for the Superstar is simply "Yes" or "No."

DO NOT SETTLE FOR LESS THAN A STAFF OF 10S WHO ARE GIVERS COMMITTED TO YOUR VISION AND ACCEPTING OF CHANGE.

After you have completed the evaluation form, proceed as follows: "John, I have reviewed your job performance, and these are the things I need." Don't say what he is doing wrong; instead, tell him what is needed. For example: "When we make a change, I need you to embrace it." "I need the alarm turned on each night." "I need customers to feel important." "I need accurate reports." "I need the office to be clean." "These are the things I need; do you think you can give them to me?"

If he says yes (and if it is appropriate) say, "Great! In thirty (or sixty or ninety) days, if this has been accomplished, you can look forward to a $X raise in pay. How is that, John?" Give him a chance to respond; and if he says "Great!" then, look him right in the eye and ask, John, are you still committed to my vision?" As with hiring, there are three answers: "Yes," "No," or "I'm not sure."

If his answer is "Yes," say thanks and send him back to work. If it's "No," give him a severance paycheck, because "I'm only going to work with people committed to my vision."

If it's "I'm not sure," push for an answer. An employee who has been working more than three months should know if he or she is committed to your vision.

Have a second meeting a few days later, and tell John all the things he is doing well. This second meeting is very important for morale, and you will often hear all the things already being done to give you what you need.

Keep a running record of your evaluations and meetings with each employee, making notes with the date and what was discussed each time.

Note: There are two other employee review forms at the end of this chapter.

The following were taken from actual employee evaluations:

- This man has delusions of adequacy.

- He sets low personal standards and consistently fails to achieve them.

- Since my last report, this employee has reached rock bottom and shows signs of starting to dig.

- His men would follow him anywhere, but only out of morbid curiosity.

- I would not allow this man to breed.

- This associate is really not so much of a has-been but more of a definitely won't be.

- When he opens his mouth, it seems that this is only to change whichever foot was previously in there.

- He would be out of his depth in a parking lot puddle.

- A room-temperature I.Q.

- One-celled organisms outscore him in I.Q. tests.

- Donated his brain to science before he was quite finished using it.

- Fell out of his family tree.

- If brains were taxed, he would get a rebate.

- Any dumber and he would have to be watered twice a week.

- If you gave him a penny for his thoughts, you would get change back.

- If you stand close enough to him, you can hear the ocean.

- It's hard to believe that his beat out one million other sperm.

- Some drink from the fountain of knowledge. He gargled.

- Got into the gene pool while the lifeguard wasn't looking.

- This employee is depriving a village somewhere of an idiot.

When you hire from your vision, These kinds of employees, Will *NEVER* show up.

EMPLOYEE COMPENSATION

"How?" "When?" and "How much?" are frequently asked questions about paying employees. Here are some guidelines to assist you in formulating your compensation package. (Be sure to comply with all state and federal regulations.)

Pay every two weeks on Friday. This allows employees to get a check on a regular basis. A payroll company is a very inexpensive and accurate way to handle payroll.

Medical Insurance is a benefit most employees need. As long as the plan is a written, non-discriminating program, it is not taxable to the employee and is deductible to the employer.

Sick pay is the continuation of wages an employee receives while temporarily absent from work because of illness or injury. Payments made during the first six months that the employee is off work are taxable to the employee.

Many businesses reimburse employees or pay them a fixed allowance to cover the expense of acquiring and maintaining a uniform. If you reimburse employees for uniform-connected expenses, and require them to account for these expenses, the reimbursements will be tax-free to employees.

You may reimburse employees who obtain the child care necessary for them to work. Reimbursements or expenses assumed must be under a written, non-discriminatory child-care program and must be for the care of children under age thirteen (or any dependent unable to care for himself or herself). Employees can exclude from taxable income up to $5,000 in a child-care assistance program.

Many employers promote employee goodwill by means of cash or non-cash gifts. Merchandise gifts (e.g., turkeys, hams, champagne, etc.) that are of nominal value are not subject to tax. Gifts of cash, or of items that are readily convertible to cash, are taxable.

Note: Hiring poor or inexperienced employees because it will cost less is usually a false savings. Successful businesses seem to go along with highly paid long-term employees.

Always complete a compensation sheet (see sample at the end of this chapter) so employees can see their total compensation.

When looking for new employees, advertise the total monthly compensation package. (See the Total Compensation form at the end of this chapter.)

CONFRONTATIONAL SITUATIONS

A few words about firing an employee—the ultimate in confrontational situations. When in a confrontational situation, come from what you want and how you feel. No one can argue with what you want and how you feel.

Example: "Judy, I want to make some changes in the business, and I feel this is not the right business for you." Then be quiet and let her respond. When she stops speaking, say, "I hear that, and I want to make some changes, and I feel this is not the right business for you."

When she hears you, she will say, "Oh." There may be tears involved, and its fine for you to cry also, but don't give her a lot of reasons, because then you have to make her wrong and make her feel bad, and she'll have all kinds of reasons why your reasons are invalid. So only come from what you want and how you feel, and when she's heard that, say, "Judy, here's a check."

Give her as much severance pay, or pay in lieu of work, as makes you feel good. That might be two weeks or two months.

Application for Employment Date_____

Name _____ Phone _____

Address _____ City_____Zip_____

Social Security #_____ Driver's License#_____

In case of an emergency, Call_____Phone_____

For payroll, how many dependents do you claim?__ DOB_____

List allergies_____

Schooling:_____

Previous Employment:

Employer_____Phone_____
        Position_____

Employer_____Phone_____
        Position_____

Employer_____Phone_____
        Position_____

Personal references, not related, whom you have known for at least one year.

Name _____ Phone #_____

Name _____ Phone #_____

Name _____ Phone #_____

I have read the manual, agreements, and dress code and I agree._____

Office notes

INDIVIDUAL EMPLOYEE EVALUATION FORM

NAME_____

POSITION_____ DATE_____

CATEGORY   RATING   WHAT IS NEEDED TO
IMPROVE?

- Overall effectiveness   _____   _____
- Unconditional commitment   _____   _____
- Giver versus Taker   _____   _____
- Offensive versus Defensive   _____   _____
- Superstar   _____   _____

Notes:

INDIVIDUAL EMPLOYEE EVALUATION FORM

NAME_____

POSITION_____ DATE_____

CATEGORY   RATING   WHAT IS NEEDED TO
IMPROVE?

- Overall effectiveness   _____   _____
- Unconditional commitment   _____   _____
- Giver versus Taker   _____   _____
- Offensive versus Defensive   _____   _____
- Superstar   _____   _____

Notes:

MASTER EMPLOYEE EVALUATION FORM

Name_____

Position_____

Overall_____

Commitment_____

Giver/Taker_____

Offensive/Defensive_____

Superstar_____

Name_____

Position_____

Overall_____

Commitment_____

Giver/Taker_____

Offensive/Defensive_____

Superstar_____

Name_____

Position_____

Overall_____

Commitment_____

Giver/Taker_____

Offensive/Defensive_____

Superstar_____

Name_____

Position_____

Overall_____

Commitment_____

Giver/Taker_____

Offensive/Defensive_____

Superstar_____

OVERALL PERFORMANCE (1–10)

 How well does he/she do the job? Overall presentation.

COMMITMENT TO THE VISION (1–10)

Willingness to do what it takes to get the job done.   "You can count on me."

GIVER OR TAKER (G or T)

The giver knows the more you give, the more you get; is an "energy giver."

The taker feels someone has to lose for him or her to win; is an "energy taker."

OFFENSIVE OR DEFENSIVE (O or D)

Offensive: Willingness to accept change.

Defensive: "I like it the way it is."

SUPERSTAR (Yes or No)

Energy must swirl around them.

GROWTH APPRAISAL AND PERFORMANCE EFFICIENCY REVIEW

Name: _____   Date: _____

RATING SCALE:

5 — Outstanding

4 — Above Average

3 — Satisfactory

2 — Needs Improvement

1 — Not Satisfactory

N/A — Not Applicable

ATTITUDE - INITIATIVE

N/A 1 2 3 4 5 Has the personal drive and determination to get the job done

N/A 1 2 3 4 5 Takes pride in accomplishment

N/A 1 2 3 4 5 Wants to do the best job possible for each task

N/A 1 2 3 4 5 Enthusiasm

TEAMWORK

N/A 1 2 3 4 5 Understands office priorities and balances own to be compatible

N/A 1 2 3 4 5 Willing to work out problems that hinder team performance; handles conflict well

N/A 1 2 3 4 5 Recognizes contributions from others

N/A 1 2 3 4 5 Seeks new ways to improve self and others

N/A 1 2 3 4 5 Trusts coworkers

N/A 1 2 3 4 5 Shares willingly: skills, knowledge and time

N/A 1 2 3 4 5 Gives and receives directions well

DEPENDABILITY

N/A Yes No   Would you give this person a task and feel confident it would get done?

N/A Yes No Are problems encountered or inability to complete a task reported to boss?

N/A Yes No Does employee give full efforts and concentration to the job?

TRAINING

N/A Yes No   Is training received being used?

N/A Yes No   Does employee use initiative to seek additional training?

N/A 1 2 3 4 5 How effective is this person in training others?

N/A Yes No   Would you want to be trained by this person?

COMMUNICATION

N/A Yes No   Are points made clearly and concisely?

N/A Yes No   Does this person contribute willingly in all office settings, including meetings?

N/A Yes No   Does this person discuss work-related problems with supervisors rather than other employees?

GENERAL PERFORMANCE

N/A 1 2 3 4 5 Well respected

N/A 1 2 3 4 5 Trusted

N/A 1 2 3 4 5 Hardworking

N/A 1 2 3 4 5 Contributing

N/A 1 2 3 4 5 Developing member

N/A 1 2 3 4 5 Open honest

N/A 1 2 3 4 5 Professional

N/A 1 2 3 4 5 Thorough

N/A 1 2 3 4 5 Active

ATTENDANCE

N/A 1 2 3 4 5 Attendance record

N/A 1 2 3 4 5 When misses has a good reason

N/A 1 2 3 4 5 Punctuality

APPEARANCE

N/A 1 2 3 4 5 Hair

N/A 1 2 3 4 5 Nails

N/A 1 2 3 4 5 Clothes

N/A 1 2 3 4 5 Overall appearance

ATTITUDE

N/A 1 2 3 4 5 Personal attitude at 8:00 a.m.

N/A 1 2 3 4 5 Personal attitude at 5:00 p.m.

N/A 1 2 3 4 5 Toward staff members leaving early

N/A 1 2 3 4 5 Manner around the office

N/A 1 2 3 4 5 Attitude with Customers

N/A 1 2 3 4 5 Attitude with other office personnel

N/A 1 2 3 4 5 Attitude with Boss

N/A 1 2 3 4 5 Attitude when given additional work

TELEPHONE

N/A 1 2 3 4 5 Answering

N/A 1 2 3 4 5 Ability to answer questions

N/A 1 2 3 4 5 Personal calls don't interfere with work

N/A 1 2 3 4 5 Private life doesn't interfere with work

FREE TIME

N/A 1 2 3 4 5 Finds things to do

N/A 1 2 3 4 5 Helpful to other staff

N/A 1 2 3 4 5 Efficiency

OVERALL RATING

1 2 3 4 5

SALARY Expects a raise: Yes __ No __

If so, how much?

EMPLOYEE/EMPLOYER REVIEW

The purpose of the employee review is to support each employee in achieving a higher level of performance. This review is therefore intended as a learning process for both employee and employer to be completed separately. Please circle the highest level you feel your employee has achieved.

1. Considering all aspects of my performance including grooming; promptness; communicating with others; attitude; skills; and my desire to grow in my position, I rate myself:

(Lowest) 1 2 3 4 5 6 7 8 9 10 (Highest)

2. For many of us, it is important that we are committed to our families, our church, and all other aspects of our lives. Besides being committed at a high level to my personal life, I rate my commitment to my position in the organization at the level of:

(Lowest) 1 2 3 4 5 6 7 8 9 10 (Highest)

3. We all know that change is sometimes difficult and that it is necessary for us to make many changes in the office. I rate my ability to change as:

| (Very difficult to make change) | 1 2 3 4 5 6 7 8 9 10 | (Easy to make change) |

4. The purpose of this office and the vision of the boss is:

| (Not very clear) | 1 2 3 4 5 6 7 8 9 10 | (Very clear) |

5. I see myself committed to the purpose and vision of this practice as follows:

| (Not very committed) | 1 2 3 4 5 6 7 8 9 10 | (Very committed) |

6. I like the position that I have in this firm at the level that I marked.

      (Dislike my position)   1 2 3 4 5 6 7 8 9 10   (Like my position)

7. All of us have interruptions during the day that tend to decrease what we can accomplish. I rate the interruptions that I have as follows:

      (Very few   1 2 3 4 5 6 7 8 9 10   (I have lots of
interruptions)   interruptions)

8. In order to be profitable, an organization must charge fees for the service it delivers. The fees that this office charges are:

      (Low)   1 2 3 4 5 6 7 8 9 10   (High)

9. Our office is committed to quality. At the present time, I see the quality we deliver as:

      (Low quality)   1 2 3 4 5 6 7 8 9 10   (High quality)

TOTAL COMPENSATION

Employee _____ Date _____

$ _____ Hourly pay

$ _____ Monthly pay

$ _____ Monthly retirement contribution

$ _____ Monthly health insurance

$ _____ Monthly uniform allowance

$ _____ Monthly child care

$ _____ Paid vacation (hourly pay x 8 hours x # days vacation, divided by 12 = paid vacation prorated monthly)

$ _____ Paid sick leave (compute like paid vacation)

$ _____ Other monthly compensation (list)

$ _____ Total monthly compensation package divided by 12

$ _____ Total yearly compensation package

Chapter 3 - THE BUSINESS

THE GATEKEEPER

A properly decorated and equipped place of business bespeaks excellence, as do well groomed, properly dressed, competent, friendly and caring employees. The first employee your customer meets will set the tone for future relations. This person carries the full responsibility of imparting a favorable first impression of your business. More importantly, perhaps, is this employee dedicated to your business and your customers? Does she make each and every person who contacts your business feel important? Is there a smile in her voice? Does she listen? She must really love what she does and at all times represent excellence and quality, because she represents your business.

THE TELEPHONE

How should your phone be answered?

"Good morning, ABC Company! This is Carole!!"

This greeting is short and friendly and delivers all the necessary information. Make sure it is not delivered "machine-gun" style, like military personnel often answer the phone. The caller must be able to understand what is being said.

What is your gatekeeper's response when someone calls and asks to speak with the boss? Here is a response that shows caring and warmth but still allows the call to be screened: "Who's calling please"? "Bill Smith." "I know she'll want to speak to you, Bill. Let me see if she can speak now."

> *Frequently used phone numbers, including the boss's home number, should be readily accessible.*

Train your gatekeeper to use the following guidelines for giving top-quality service to every caller and customers visiting your business.

Look at things from the customer's point of view. Dealing with your business should be pleasing and comfortable. Your tone and manner should always overshadow your technical performance. Put yourself in the customer's shoes, and treat each and every caller with respect. Customers react favorably to a gatekeeper who shows an interest in satisfying their needs. Engage the customer in natural conversation to establish a personal rapport and heighten credibility.

Make a point of using the customer's name during your conversation.

Convey enthusiasm, smile when you answer the phone, offer a friendly greeting, and beware of sounding tired or bored, even toward the end of a tiring day.

Show empathy with a customer's problem by using expressions such as, "I understand."

Pay attention, even though you may have heard the same complaint from a number of previous customers.

Make every customer feel that he or she rates as one of your company's best customers.

<u>What Your Voice Says About You</u>

In face-to-face encounters, much of your communication, according to experts, is done through body language: eye contact, hand gestures, body movement, and facial expressions. On the telephone, all that is lost, so you have to work twice as hard to communicate. One way to personalize telephone contact is by using the caller's name.

Put a smile in your voice. No matter how positive and convincing what you have to say is, it's how you say it that puts it across. Begin by putting a smile on your face, literally! It makes a world of difference. Your voice will come across as lively and enthusiastic.

Slow down. At the beginning of the call, speak a little more slowly than you normally would. In most cases, this makes it easier for people to concentrate on and understand what you are saying. If it reaches the point where your caller is speaking at a much faster or slower rate than you are, then alter your speed accordingly.

Enunciate your words. English is full of similar sounds like "t" and "d" and "p" and "b." Don't make the person struggle to understand you or to have to ask you to repeat something. Clarify by saying, "Is that *t* as in *Tom* or *d* as in *David?*" You should never talk with food, gum, or a pencil in your mouth.

Be courteous. Courtesy is demonstrating respect and consideration for the caller by being friendly, polite, and positive. It also includes responding to his needs and demonstrating a willingness to help. Courtesy requires being patient with each caller, showing consideration and good manners, expressing regret or concern when appropriate, and responding or acting in a manner that reflects interest in the customer's needs and concerns.

Listen to what your caller is saying. Listening is the active process of being attentive to the customer throughout the call. Listening is the part of communication many people overlook. Effective listening means giving full attention to what the customer is saying and focusing on and documenting the key details of his questions. It also means clarifying what the customer has said by repeating the content and asking relevant questions, without interrupting him.

Listen to your own voice. Always remember that to the person on the line, you are the business. In today's competitive environment, you need your customer to rely on the services or products you provide. Only by developing loyalty through top-quality service will you continue to be successful and grow. Remember, your voice is painting the mental picture that the caller is forming of you that reflects the business and entire staff. *You never have a second chance to make a first impression!* You are making that first impression of the business to a lot of different people—it's an important job!

MORE FOOD FOR THOUGHT

Ever wonder why customers leave your **business**? According to *U.S. News and World Report:*

> 4 percent— Move
>
> 5 percent—Have a friend in he business
>
> 9 percent—Price
>
> 14 percent— Dissatisfaction with product or service
>
> *68—PERCENT INDIFFERENCE BY SOMEONE AT THE BUSINESS*

EXPECTATIONS

When a customer or potential customer approaches your place of business, what are his expectations? Are the expectations something he assumed he should expect? Or are his expectations something he was told he should expect? Or are his expectations what you declared he could expect?

I suggest that you tell customers in plain language what they can expect from your business, and then deliver it. Establish standards that strongly imply, "That's just the way we do business." This creates a controlled expectation in the customer.

Customers are lost because their expectations are not met. Tell them what they can expect, and then deliver. Enlist them to put their names on your mailbox.

BECAUSE THE CUSTOMER

Because the customer
has a *need*,
we have a job to do.

Because the customer
has a choice,
we must be the *better choice*.

Because the customer
has sensibilities,
we must be *considerate*.

Because the customer
has an urgency,
we must be *quick*.

Because the customer
is unique,
we must be *flexible*.

Because the customer
has high expectations,
we must *excel*.

Because the customer
has *influence*,
we have the hope of
more customers.

Because of the customer,
we *exist*!

NEED I SAY MORE?

THE REFERRAL BUSINESS

So many times we have heard the following statement: "The best client is one who is referred by another client." And it is generally a true statement, because clients are our friends. When a friend refers a friend, she has a sincerity that cannot be faked, and that sincerity comes across to whoever she is talking to.

Let's face it: all businesses are referral businesses. In this age of electronic advertising, direct mail, yellow pages, and discounts, how do you get your customers to become your friend and refer new customers to you?

Four Steps to Nurturing Customers and Building a Referral Business:

1. Treat all customers as honored guests in your business. The moment a human being enters your business, put aside any paperwork you are doing, move your attention away from your computer, and cease personal

conversations with other employees. Be genuinely happy to see your customer. Call her by name. Have a warm, loving, caring attitude in your **business**. Remember the old retailer's adage "The customer is always right." Always go the extra mile. People enjoy happy, friendly places where they are made to feel special and important.

2. Keep accurate track of all endorsements. Ask each new customer, "Whom can I thank for referring you to us?" This lets the new customer know right away that you want and appreciate referrals. Ask this question instead of having her write it down, so you can discuss her answer with her.

3. Let your client know you are a referral **business** and you appreciate her endorsement. Ask your customer if she would be willing to refer to you. Give her a couple of your business cards. When she does refer someone to you, mark her file with a bright sticker and write down the name and date of the referral so you can thank her at your next contact.

4. Acknowledge each referral. When you are referred a customer, think of that referral as a gift, a very expensive gift. Also, the person making the referral went out on a limb for you and that took an act of faith on her part. Acknowledge this act with a personalized, handwritten note. Computer-written letters are fine, but a handwritten note really shows your appreciation.

You create a referral business by becoming friends with your customers and letting them know how much you appreciate their endorsement. Start today. The rewards, both tangible and intangible, are enormous.

RELATIONSHIPS

Having good relationships with people involves being with people in a way that serves their needs fully. It is providing more than is expected. It begins with a commitment to excellence in everything you do.

The boss commits to being a 10 and unconditionally commits to the vision. The employees commit to being 10s and unconditionally commit to the vision. The business is a 10 across the board. When the boss recognizes herself as a 10, and the employees recognizes the boss and the business as 10s, the business flourishes.

Treating customers well causes them to return, and pays off in referrals of new customers.

GOLDEN POINTS OF SERVICE

Michael LeBoeuf, in his Nightingale Conant tape, *Insight*, discusses the five most important ingredients to providing the type of service that keeps customers coming back:

1. RELIABILITY: Be "count-on-able." Be consistent. People want to know what to expect. Repeat business and referrals will rise as people see consistency in your service.

2. CREDIBILITY: Have the best interests of the customer at heart. She wants security and integrity. She does *not* want *risk, danger,* or *doubt.*

3. ATTRACTIVENESS: See the boss, the business, and the employees through the eyes of a client. Do you look good? Does that look bespeak quality? Looks can deceive, but it's better to look sharp than shabby.

4. RESPONSIVENESS: Be on time. Be available. Take care of problems promptly at no extra cost. Emergencies must be handled quickly and completely.

5. EMPATHY: Every customer is unique, with special needs, wants, and problems. Successful businesses treat customers as individuals.

These are the golden points of service. They are how your business is judged. Post them where all employees can see them.

STAFF MEETINGS

A recent survey found that most businesses did not have regularly scheduled staff meetings. Many had meetings "when they are needed." Those offices run on a "management by crisis" style. A better management style is one that involves planning and regular communication. Meetings help communication as long as they have a stated purpose and an intended result.

"People support what they help create."

There are basically seven types of meetings. They are: 1) The Huddle; 2) The Closing; 3) The Time-Out; 4) The Regular; 5) The Training; 6) The Appraisal; and 7) The Year-End. Let's discuss each one.

The Huddle is the best way to start each day. It begins fifteen minutes before the first customer is due and lasts no more than ten minutes. The Huddle has five parts:

1. Read the mission statement for the business. This gets everyone refocused on "why we are here." Employees should take turns reading it aloud.

2. Is a production goal scheduled? If not, what will you do to increase production?

3. Review all customers coming in today.

4. Which customers will you ask for referrals and who will do it?

5. Review the records to see where you are in relation to your goals for the month.

6. Who needs support today? Don't start the day with employees who are not at their best. Come together as a team to help and support one another.

This meeting should be a happy and upbeat time, with only positive subjects discussed.

The Closing Meeting is held in order to be sure that each employee leaves the business complete. All communications are delivered so no problems are carried home. This meeting should last two to ten minutes and begin as soon as the last customer leaves the business.

The Time-Out Meeting is called by anyone any time the day is falling apart for him. This may be a business crisis or a personal crisis. The purpose is to give the employee in crisis a chance to ask for support. This should take only a minute or two, allowing the stressed individual to get back to normal and resume his team duties.

The Regular Meeting is for problem solving and for relaying information that can't be communicated during the regular work day. It should be firmly scheduled, with no interruptions, at least monthly, and, if there is a lot to accomplish, weekly. In very well run businesses, weekly regular meetings may be too often. Have an agenda and use it. Post an agenda where employees can access it so that they can list their own items to be discussed.

This is a good time to have one employee tell everyone else about what he does in the business. Most of us don't know what our coworkers really do to contribute to the team effort. Periodically, ask an employee to stand and have everyone else acknowledge the good things about this person. We all love to be acknowledged, even though at first it seems embarrassing.

The Training Meeting is held to create experts in each area of the business and then to cross-train every other employee. It is scheduled as needed. Have an outline of what is to be taught and tape it either by audio or video, so that a record is available for future study. Put only one subject on each tape.

The Appraisal Meeting is used to properly communicate privately and individually to employees the areas in which they need improvement, and to acknowledge all their positive attributes. This is handled in two meetings, regularly scheduled, in a comfortable, quiet atmosphere, with adequate time allowed.

At the first meeting, go over areas that employees need to improve. Be specific and give them a time limit for improvement. At the second meeting, held two to four days later, tell them everything they do well, listing all their positive attributes. Because of the atmosphere this creates, employees often will tell you the steps they have already taken to accomplish what was needed from meeting number one. This is the meeting that cements them to you.

The Year-End Meeting covers the following topics:

1. What the business has accomplished during the last year
2. What has not been working
3. Goals for the new year
4. Successes of this past year
5. Each person's contribution

Be sure that with the Regular, Training, Appraisal, and Year-End meetings, a written record is kept of what was decided or accomplished, and at the end of each meeting, sum up the results.

When employees were asked what they wanted from a job, two of the top three items were "appreciation of good work" and "feeling in on things." Staff meetings, properly thought out and well run, will help to give employees what they want.

Carefully evaluate your business, and decide how staff meetings can be incorporated into your routine.

THE BUSINESS PLAN

You now understand why you started your business; you understand your role; you understand the role of employees; now you put it all together into a plan for your business.

The business plan is divided into the following steps:

- Create a vision statement. It is the basis of the plan. Everything flows from the vision.

- List core values.

- State the agreements.

- List how the business will be advertised.

- Develop a pro forma budget.

- Design monitors that show how the business is doing.

- Create a business manual. It should begin by stating the purpose of the office, or the vision. Then it should describe how the office will function. Be sure to include the business policy concerning compensation and raises, health insurance, vacations, holidays, sick leave. Modify and add to these subjects to fit your business.

GENERAL OFFICE POLICIES

VISION:

AGREEMENTS:

COMPENSATION:

HEALTH INSURANCE:

VACATIONS:

SICK LEAVE:

HOLIDAYS:

MEETINGS:

There you have it.
Never forget that it's your business.
Now do something about it.
Have fun and good luck.